Super Fast Fat Burning Cookbook

Quick and Delicious Recipes to Ignite Your Metabolism and Shed
Pounds Fast

Blake Vanover

Super Fast Fat Burning Cookbook

Introduction

Welcome to the *Super Fast Fat Burning Cookbook.* This cookbook is designed for those who want to quickly and efficiently shed unwanted pounds without spending hours in the kitchen. Whether you're a busy professional, a parent on the go, or someone just starting your fat loss journey, these recipes will help you boost your metabolism and burn fat faster than ever before.

In this introduction, we'll cover the science of fat burning, why speed matters, and how to make the most of this cookbook. Plus, we'll share some essential tips that will set you up for success on your fat-burning journey.

The Science Behind Fat Burning

Before we dive into the recipes, let's take a quick look at how fat burning works. Our bodies burn fat as fuel, especially when we engage in physical activity or consume the right foods that help rev up our metabolism. When your metabolism is working at full capacity, your body burns more calories, even when you're at rest.

Certain foods, like those high in protein, healthy fats, and fiber, are known to help increase metabolism. These foods also keep you feeling full for longer, preventing overeating and helping you stick to your fat-burning goals. In this book, you'll find recipes that focus on these metabolism-boosting foods, ensuring you stay energized and satisfied throughout the day.

Why Speed Matters in Fat Loss

We all know the importance of consistent exercise, but what many people overlook is the role that fast, efficient meals play in fat loss. The idea behind this cookbook is that by preparing meals quickly without sacrificing nutritional value, you can stay on track with your fat-burning goals even on your busiest days.

The recipes in this book are designed to be prepared in 30 minutes or less, allowing you to enjoy flavorful, healthy meals without having to spend hours cooking or meal prepping. These quick meals also ensure that you can maintain a sustainable, long-term eating plan, rather than turning to quick fixes that are often unhealthy and unsustainable.

How to Use This Cookbook for Maximum Results

This cookbook is more than just a collection of recipes—it's a guide to creating healthy, balanced meals that will help you burn fat fast. Here's how you can get the most out of it:

1. **Choose a Variety of Recipes**: In each chapter, you'll find a mix of breakfast, lunch, dinner, snack, and drink recipes. We've made sure there are plenty of options for every meal, so you can enjoy variety without feeling restricted. Eating a variety of foods is important for long-term fat loss because it keeps your meals interesting and satisfying.

2. **Use the Meal Prep Tips**: In Chapter 6, we've included meal prep ideas to help you get ahead of your week. Meal prepping allows you to save time while ensuring that you always have healthy, fat-burning meals ready to go.

3. **Incorporate Exercise**: While the recipes in this book are designed to speed up fat burning, exercise is still an important part of any fat-loss journey. Incorporating regular movement—whether it's walking, strength training, or high-intensity interval training—will complement your fat-burning meals and help you see faster results.

4. **Stay Consistent**: Consistency is key to long-term fat loss. The recipes in this cookbook are designed to be quick and easy, so you'll be more likely to stick to your healthy eating habits. Don't be discouraged by setbacks—fat loss takes time, and each small, healthy choice adds up.

Helpful Tips for Success

Here are some bonus tips to help you stay on track and make the most of this cookbook:

- **Stay Hydrated**: Drinking enough water is essential for fat loss. Water helps flush toxins from your body, keeps your metabolism running smoothly, and keeps you feeling full between meals.

- **Use the Right Cooking Methods**: When preparing meals, try methods like grilling, steaming, or baking instead of frying. These cooking techniques preserve the nutrients in the food and minimize the use of unhealthy fats.

- **Mind Your Portions**: While all the recipes in this cookbook are healthy, portion control is still important. Make sure you're eating the right portion sizes to maintain a calorie deficit, which is essential for fat loss.

- **Balance Your Macros**: Fat loss is about finding the right balance of protein, carbs, and fats in your meals. Each recipe in this cookbook is designed to help you hit that balance, but don't forget to listen to your body and adjust portions based on your individual needs.

Conclusion

This cookbook is not just a guide to quick meals; it's a tool to help you achieve a healthier, fitter version of yourself. By focusing on fast, fat-burning recipes that you can prepare in minutes, you're taking a significant step toward reaching your fitness goals without complicated diets or hours of meal prep. Get ready to ignite your metabolism, burn fat, and enjoy delicious, satisfying meals every day.

Now, let's get started with the recipes that will help you transform your body and your life!

Chapter 1: Breakfast Boosters (7 Fast Fat-Burning Breakfasts)

Starting your day with a metabolism-boosting breakfast is crucial to kick-start your fat-burning process. A balanced breakfast sets the tone for the rest of the day, keeps you full, and prevents cravings that can derail your fat loss goals. The recipes in this chapter are designed to be quick, easy, and packed with nutrients to fuel your body, rev up your metabolism, and keep you satisfied until your next meal.

1. Protein-Packed Green Smoothie

Prep time: 5 minutes
Cook time: 0 minutes
Total time: 5 minutes

Ingredients:

- 1 cup spinach

- 1/2 avocado

- 1 cup unsweetened almond milk

- 1 scoop protein powder (vanilla or chocolate)

- 1 tbsp chia seeds

- Ice cubes (optional)

Instructions:

1. Add all ingredients into a blender.

2. Blend until smooth and creamy.

3. Pour into a glass and enjoy immediately.

Nutritional Info:

- Calories: 250

- Fat: 18g

- Carbs: 10g

- Protein: 20g

2. Egg & Veggie Scramble

Prep time: 5 minutes
Cook time: 7 minutes
Total time: 12 minutes

Ingredients:

- 3 large eggs

- 1/4 cup diced bell pepper

- 1/4 cup spinach

- 1 tbsp olive oil

- Salt and pepper to taste

Instructions:

1. Heat olive oil in a pan over medium heat.

2. Add diced bell pepper and spinach, sauté for 2-3 minutes.

3. Crack eggs into the pan and scramble until cooked through.

4. Season with salt and pepper, then serve.

Nutritional Info:

- Calories: 300

- Fat: 22g

- Carbs: 7g

- Protein: 21g

3. Low-Carb Avocado Toast

Prep time: 5 minutes
Cook time: 0 minutes
Total time: 5 minutes

Ingredients:

- 1 slice whole grain or keto-friendly bread

- 1/2 avocado

- 1 tbsp lemon juice

- Salt and pepper to taste

- Red pepper flakes (optional)

Instructions:

1. Toast the bread to your liking.

2. Mash avocado with lemon juice, salt, and pepper.

3. Spread the avocado mixture onto the toasted bread.

4. Top with red pepper flakes for a kick, if desired.

Nutritional Info:

- Calories: 230

- Fat: 15g

- Carbs: 20g

- Protein: 4g

4. Chia Seed Pudding with Almond Butter

Prep time: 5 minutes
Cook time: 0 minutes (overnight prep)
Total time: 5 minutes

Ingredients:

- 1/4 cup chia seeds

- 1 cup unsweetened almond milk

- 1 tbsp almond butter

- 1 tsp vanilla extract

- Stevia or honey (optional)

Instructions:

1. In a bowl, mix chia seeds, almond milk, and vanilla extract.

2. Stir in almond butter, and sweeten with stevia or honey if desired.

3. Refrigerate overnight.

4. Stir again in the morning and enjoy.

Nutritional Info:

- Calories: 300

- Fat: 22g

- Carbs: 18g

- Protein: 12g

5. Greek Yogurt Parfait with Berries and Nuts

Prep time: 5 minutes
Cook time: 0 minutes
Total time: 5 minutes

Ingredients:

- 1 cup Greek yogurt (unsweetened)

- 1/4 cup mixed berries (strawberries, blueberries, raspberries)

- 2 tbsp mixed nuts (almonds, walnuts)

- 1 tsp chia seeds

Instructions:

1. In a bowl, layer Greek yogurt, berries, and nuts.

2. Sprinkle chia seeds on top.

3. Serve immediately for a quick, protein-packed breakfast.

Nutritional Info:

- Calories: 280

- Fat: 18g

- Carbs: 15g

- Protein: 20g

6. Banana Almond Pancakes (Low-Carb)

Prep time: 5 minutes
Cook time: 7 minutes
Total time: 12 minutes

Ingredients:

- 1 ripe banana, mashed

- 2 eggs

- 1/4 cup almond flour

- 1/2 tsp baking powder

- 1/4 tsp cinnamon

- 1 tbsp almond butter (for topping)

Instructions:

1. In a bowl, whisk together the mashed banana, eggs, almond flour, baking powder, and cinnamon.

2. Heat a pan over medium heat and lightly grease with coconut oil or butter.

3. Pour the batter into small pancakes and cook for about 2-3 minutes per side.

4. Top with almond butter before serving.

Nutritional Info:

- Calories: 250

- Fat: 18g

- Carbs: 18g

- Protein: 8g

7. Flaxseed & Spinach Breakfast Muffins

Prep time: 10 minutes
Cook time: 15 minutes
Total time: 25 minutes

Ingredients:

- 1 cup almond flour

- 1/4 cup flaxseed meal

- 1 cup spinach, finely chopped

- 2 eggs

- 1/4 cup unsweetened almond milk

- 1 tsp baking powder

- Salt and pepper to taste

Instructions:

1. Preheat the oven to 350°F (175°C) and grease a muffin tin.

2. In a bowl, mix almond flour, flaxseed meal, spinach, baking powder, salt, and pepper.

3. Add eggs and almond milk, then stir until combined.

4. Pour the batter into the muffin tin and bake for 15 minutes or until a toothpick comes out clean.

5. Allow to cool and enjoy!

Nutritional Info:

- Calories: 150

- Fat: 12g

- Carbs: 8g

- Protein: 8g

These breakfast recipes are designed to help you fuel your day, support your fat-burning goals, and keep you full longer. Each one is easy to prepare, filled with metabolism-boosting ingredients, and packed with nutrients to start your day right. Enjoy these tasty and healthy options while keeping your body in fat-burning mode!

Chapter 2: Power-Packed Lunches

Lunch is a critical meal that helps sustain your energy levels throughout the day, prevent mid-afternoon cravings, and keep your metabolism revving. The recipes in this chapter are designed to give you a power-packed punch of nutrients, protein, and healthy fats to keep you feeling satisfied and burning fat efficiently. These quick meals can be made in under 30 minutes and are ideal for busy individuals who want to eat healthy without spending hours in the kitchen.

1. Grilled Chicken & Quinoa Salad

Prep time: 10 minutes
Cook time: 15 minutes
Total time: 25 minutes

Ingredients:

- 1 boneless, skinless chicken breast

- 1/2 cup quinoa (uncooked)

- 1 cup mixed salad greens (spinach, arugula, etc.)

- 1/4 cup cucumber, diced

- 1/4 cup cherry tomatoes, halved

- 1 tbsp olive oil

- 1 tbsp lemon juice

- Salt and pepper to taste

Instructions:

1. Cook quinoa according to package instructions.

2. Season chicken breast with salt, pepper, and a drizzle of olive oil. Grill for 6-7 minutes per side until fully cooked.

3. In a large bowl, toss together salad greens, cucumber, tomatoes, and cooked quinoa.

4. Slice the grilled chicken and top the salad with it.

5. Drizzle with lemon juice and a bit more olive oil before serving.

Nutritional Info:

- Calories: 350

- Fat: 14g

- Carbs: 30g

- Protein: 30g

2. Zucchini Noodles with Pesto & Grilled Shrimp

Prep time: 10 minutes
Cook time: 10 minutes
Total time: 20 minutes

Ingredients:

- 2 medium zucchinis, spiralized into noodles

- 6 oz shrimp, peeled and deveined

- 2 tbsp pesto (store-bought or homemade)

- 1 tbsp olive oil

- Salt and pepper to taste

- 1/2 tbsp parmesan cheese (optional)

Instructions:

1. Heat olive oil in a skillet over medium heat. Season shrimp with salt and pepper and cook for 2-3 minutes per side, until pink and cooked through.

2. Meanwhile, sauté zucchini noodles in the same pan for 2-3 minutes until slightly softened.

3. Toss the zucchini noodles with pesto until well coated.

4. Plate the noodles, top with grilled shrimp, and sprinkle with parmesan (optional).

Nutritional Info:

- Calories: 280

- Fat: 14g

- Carbs: 8g

- Protein: 30g

3. Spinach & Salmon Bowl with Avocado

Prep time: 10 minutes
Cook time: 5 minutes
Total time: 15 minutes

Ingredients:

- 1 salmon fillet

- 1 cup fresh spinach

- 1/2 avocado, sliced

- 1 tbsp olive oil

- 1 tbsp lemon juice

- Salt and pepper to taste

Instructions:

1. Heat olive oil in a pan over medium heat. Season the salmon fillet with salt and pepper and cook for 3-4 minutes per side until golden brown and cooked through.

2. While the salmon cooks, toss fresh spinach with lemon juice.

3. Assemble the bowl by placing the spinach, sliced avocado, and cooked salmon together. Drizzle with a bit more olive oil if desired.

Nutritional Info:

- Calories: 400

- Fat: 28g

- Carbs: 10g

- Protein: 35g

4. Cauliflower Rice Stir-Fry with Tofu

Prep time: 10 minutes
Cook time: 10 minutes
Total time: 20 minutes

Ingredients:

- 1 cup cauliflower rice (store-bought or homemade)

- 1/2 cup firm tofu, cubed

- 1/4 cup bell peppers, diced

- 1/4 cup carrots, julienned

- 1 tbsp soy sauce (low-sodium)

- 1 tbsp sesame oil

- 1 tbsp green onions, chopped (for garnish)

Instructions:

1. Heat sesame oil in a pan over medium heat. Add tofu cubes and cook until crispy on all sides, about 5-7 minutes.

2. Add the bell peppers and carrots to the pan and sauté for another 2-3 minutes.

3. Stir in cauliflower rice and soy sauce, cooking for another 3-4 minutes until heated through.

4. Garnish with chopped green onions and serve.

Nutritional Info:

- Calories: 250

- Fat: 16g

- Carbs: 14g

- Protein: 18g

5. Tuna Salad Lettuce Wraps

Prep time: 5 minutes
Cook time: 0 minutes
Total time: 5 minutes

Ingredients:

- 1 can tuna in water, drained

- 2 tbsp Greek yogurt

- 1 tbsp Dijon mustard

- 1 tbsp red onion, finely chopped

- 1/4 cup celery, diced

- 1 tsp lemon juice

- 4 large lettuce leaves (for wrapping)

- Salt and pepper to taste

Instructions:

1. In a bowl, mix the tuna, Greek yogurt, Dijon mustard, red onion, celery, and lemon juice.

2. Season with salt and pepper to taste.

3. Spoon the mixture into lettuce leaves and wrap them up like a taco. Serve immediately.

Nutritional Info:

- Calories: 220

- Fat: 10g

- Carbs: 6g

- Protein: 30g

6. Cucumber & Turkey Roll-Ups

Prep time: 5 minutes
Cook time: 0 minutes
Total time: 5 minutes

Ingredients:

- 4 slices turkey breast (deli-style)

- 1/2 cucumber, thinly sliced

- 1 tbsp cream cheese (light)

- Salt and pepper to taste

Instructions:

1. Lay out the turkey slices and spread a thin layer of cream cheese on each.

2. Place the cucumber slices in the center of the turkey slice.

3. Roll them up tightly and secure with toothpicks.

4. Season with salt and pepper before serving.

Nutritional Info:

- Calories: 180

- Fat: 10g

- Carbs: 4g

- Protein: 22g

7. Chickpea & Cucumber Salad with Lemon Dressing

Prep time: 10 minutes
Cook time: 0 minutes
Total time: 10 minutes

Ingredients:

- 1 can chickpeas, drained and rinsed

- 1 cucumber, diced

- 1/4 cup red onion, chopped

- 1 tbsp lemon juice

- 1 tbsp olive oil

- Salt and pepper to taste

- Fresh parsley for garnish

Instructions:

1. In a bowl, combine chickpeas, cucumber, and red onion.

2. In a small bowl, whisk together lemon juice, olive oil, salt, and pepper.

3. Pour the dressing over the salad and toss to combine.

4. Garnish with fresh parsley before serving.

Nutritional Info:

- Calories: 220

- Fat: 12g

- Carbs: 24g

- Protein: 8g

These lunch recipes are not only quick and easy but also designed to maximize fat burning and keep you satisfied until dinner. Whether you're at work, home, or on the go, these meals are sure to support your weight loss goals while giving you the energy to power through the rest of your day. Enjoy!

Chapter 3: Energizing Dinners

Dinner is the final meal of the day, and it's essential to keep your metabolism high to continue burning fat while you sleep. These quick, satisfying dinner recipes will help you wind down the day without overloading your body with calories before bed. They focus on lean proteins, healthy fats, and plenty of vegetables—perfect for enhancing fat loss while promoting overall health. Each meal can be made in 30 minutes or less, making them perfect for those busy evenings.

1. Baked Lemon Herb Salmon with Asparagus

Prep time: 10 minutes
Cook time: 15 minutes
Total time: 25 minutes

Ingredients:

- 2 salmon fillets

- 1 tbsp olive oil

- 1 lemon, thinly sliced

- 1 bunch asparagus, trimmed

- Salt and pepper to taste

- 1 tbsp fresh dill, chopped (optional)

Instructions:

1. Preheat the oven to 400°F (200°C).

2. Place the salmon fillets on a baking sheet lined with parchment paper. Drizzle with olive oil and season with salt and pepper.

3. Arrange the lemon slices on top of the salmon fillets and surround with asparagus.

4. Bake for 15 minutes, or until salmon is cooked through and flakes easily with a fork.

5. Sprinkle with fresh dill before serving.

Nutritional Info:

- Calories: 350

- Fat: 20g

- Carbs: 8g

- Protein: 35g

2. Zucchini & Chicken Fajita Stir-Fry

Prep time: 10 minutes
Cook time: 10 minutes
Total time: 20 minutes

Ingredients:

- 2 chicken breasts, sliced into thin strips

- 2 zucchinis, sliced into rounds

- 1 bell pepper, sliced

- 1/2 onion, sliced

- 1 tbsp olive oil

- 1 tsp cumin

- 1 tsp chili powder

- 1/2 tsp garlic powder

- Salt and pepper to taste

Instructions:

1. Heat olive oil in a large skillet over medium-high heat.

2. Add the chicken and cook for 5-6 minutes until browned and cooked through.

3. Add the zucchini, bell pepper, and onion to the skillet and cook for an additional 4-5 minutes, until vegetables are tender.

4. Season with cumin, chili powder, garlic powder, salt, and pepper. Stir to combine.

5. Serve immediately.

Nutritional Info:

- Calories: 300

- Fat: 15g

- Carbs: 12g

- Protein: 30g

3. Beef & Broccoli Stir-Fry with Ginger Garlic Sauce

Prep time: 10 minutes
Cook time: 10 minutes
Total time: 20 minutes

Ingredients:

- 1 lb flank steak, thinly sliced

- 2 cups broccoli florets

- 2 tbsp soy sauce (low-sodium)

- 1 tbsp honey

- 1 tbsp ginger, minced

- 2 garlic cloves, minced

- 1 tbsp sesame oil

- 1 tsp sesame seeds (optional)

Instructions:

1. In a small bowl, combine soy sauce, honey, ginger, and garlic to make the sauce.

2. Heat sesame oil in a large skillet over medium-high heat.

3. Add the sliced beef and cook for 3-4 minutes, until browned.

4. Add the broccoli and stir-fry for another 4-5 minutes, until tender.

5. Pour the sauce over the beef and broccoli, stirring to coat evenly.

6. Sprinkle with sesame seeds before serving.

Nutritional Info:

- Calories: 350

- Fat: 20g

- Carbs: 15g

- Protein: 35g

4. Spaghetti Squash Primavera with Grilled Chicken

Prep time: 10 minutes
Cook time: 15 minutes
Total time: 25 minutes

Ingredients:

- 1 small spaghetti squash

- 2 chicken breasts, grilled and sliced

- 1 cup cherry tomatoes, halved

- 1/4 cup basil, chopped

- 1/4 cup Parmesan cheese

- 1 tbsp olive oil

- Salt and pepper to taste

Instructions:

1. Preheat the oven to 400°F (200°C). Cut the spaghetti squash in half lengthwise and remove the seeds.

2. Drizzle olive oil over the squash halves, season with salt and pepper, and place face-down on a baking sheet.

3. Roast for 20 minutes, then scrape the insides with a fork to create spaghetti-like strands.

4. Toss the squash strands with grilled chicken, cherry tomatoes, basil, and Parmesan cheese.

5. Serve immediately.

Nutritional Info:

- Calories: 350

- Fat: 15g

- Carbs: 20g

- Protein: 30g

5. Crispy Baked Shrimp with Avocado Salsa

Prep time: 10 minutes
Cook time: 10 minutes
Total time: 20 minutes

Ingredients:

- 1 lb large shrimp, peeled and deveined

- 1/2 cup breadcrumbs (whole wheat or almond flour for lower carbs)

- 1 tbsp olive oil

- 1/2 tsp paprika

- 1/4 tsp garlic powder

- 1 avocado, diced

- 1/2 cup cherry tomatoes, diced

- 1/4 cup cilantro, chopped

- 1 tbsp lime juice

Instructions:

1. Preheat the oven to 400°F (200°C). Toss the shrimp in olive oil, paprika, and garlic powder, then coat in breadcrumbs.

2. Place the shrimp on a baking sheet lined with parchment paper and bake for 8-10 minutes, until crispy and cooked

through.

3. While the shrimp bakes, mix together the avocado, tomatoes, cilantro, and lime juice to make the salsa.

4. Serve the shrimp with the avocado salsa on top.

Nutritional Info:

- Calories: 280

- Fat: 18g

- Carbs: 15g

- Protein: 25g

6. Turkey Meatballs with Cauliflower Mash

Prep time: 10 minutes
Cook time: 15 minutes
Total time: 25 minutes

Ingredients:

- 1 lb ground turkey

- 1 egg

- 1/4 cup almond flour

- 1/2 tsp garlic powder

- 1/2 tsp onion powder

- Salt and pepper to taste

- 1 small head cauliflower, chopped

- 1 tbsp butter

- 1/4 cup milk (unsweetened almond milk for low-carb)

Instructions:

1. Preheat the oven to 375°F (190°C). In a bowl, mix the ground turkey, egg, almond flour, garlic powder, onion powder, salt, and pepper.

2. Form the mixture into meatballs and place them on a baking sheet.

3. Bake for 12-15 minutes, until the meatballs are fully cooked.

4. Meanwhile, steam the cauliflower until soft. Mash with butter and milk until smooth.

5. Serve the turkey meatballs with cauliflower mash on the side.

Nutritional Info:

- Calories: 320

- Fat: 20g

- Carbs: 12g

- Protein: 30g

7. One-Pan Roasted Vegetables & Grilled Steak

Prep time: 10 minutes
Cook time: 15 minutes
Total time: 25 minutes

Ingredients:

- 2 sirloin steaks

- 1 cup Brussels sprouts, halved

- 1 cup carrots, sliced

- 1 tbsp olive oil

- 1 tbsp balsamic vinegar

- Salt and pepper to taste

Instructions:

1. Preheat the oven to 400°F (200°C). Toss the Brussels sprouts and carrots with olive oil, balsamic vinegar, salt, and pepper.

2. Spread the vegetables on a baking sheet and place the steaks on top.

3. Roast in the oven for 12-15 minutes, or until the steak reaches your desired level of doneness and the vegetables are tender.

4. Let the steak rest for a few minutes before slicing and serving with the roasted vegetables.

Nutritional Info:

- Calories: 380

- Fat: 24g

- Carbs: 20g

- Protein: 35g

These energizing dinner recipes are not only quick but also designed to support fat burning while keeping you satisfied. Whether you're looking to enjoy a juicy steak, crispy shrimp, or a healthy veggie stir-fry, these dinners are packed with the right nutrients to help you lose fat efficiently without sacrificing flavor. Enjoy these easy, flavorful meals that will leave you feeling great and energized!

Super Fast Fat Burning Cookbook

Chapter 4: Snacks That Work

Snacks can be the secret weapon in your fat-burning journey. When chosen wisely, snacks can curb hunger between meals, prevent overeating, and fuel your metabolism. The key is to choose nutrient-dense, metabolism-boosting snacks that keep you satisfied without derailing your progress. In this chapter, you'll find seven quick, easy, and delicious snacks that will keep you on track with your fat loss goals.

1. Protein-Packed Greek Yogurt with Chia Seeds

Prep time: 5 minutes
Cook time: 0 minutes
Total time: 5 minutes

Ingredients:

- 1/2 cup unsweetened Greek yogurt

- 1 tbsp chia seeds

- 1 tbsp honey or stevia (optional)

- 1/4 cup mixed berries (optional)

Instructions:

1. Scoop the Greek yogurt into a bowl.

2. Top with chia seeds, honey or stevia (if desired), and mixed berries.

3. Stir to combine and enjoy immediately.

Nutritional Info:

- Calories: 150

- Fat: 8g

- Carbs: 15g

- Protein: 10g

2. Cinnamon Almond Energy Balls

Prep time: 10 minutes
Cook time: 0 minutes
Total time: 10 minutes

Ingredients:

- 1 cup almonds, chopped

- 1/2 cup unsweetened coconut flakes

- 1/4 cup almond butter

- 1 tbsp honey

- 1/2 tsp cinnamon

- 1/4 tsp vanilla extract

Instructions:

1. In a food processor, blend almonds, coconut flakes, almond butter, honey, cinnamon, and vanilla until a sticky dough forms.

2. Roll the dough into small balls, about 1 inch in diameter.

3. Store in the fridge for a quick grab-and-go snack.

Nutritional Info:

- Calories: 180

- Fat: 14g

- Carbs: 10g

- Protein: 6g

3. Carrot Sticks with Hummus

Prep time: 5 minutes
Cook time: 0 minutes
Total time: 5 minutes

Ingredients:

- 1 medium carrot, cut into sticks

- 1/4 cup hummus (store-bought or homemade)

Instructions:

1. Peel and cut the carrot into thin sticks.

2. Serve with a small bowl of hummus for dipping.

Nutritional Info:

- Calories: 120

- Fat: 7g

- Carbs: 14g

- Protein: 3g

4. Avocado & Tomato Toast on Whole Wheat

Prep time: 5 minutes
Cook time: 5 minutes
Total time: 10 minutes

Ingredients:

- 1 slice whole wheat bread

- 1/2 avocado, mashed

- 1/4 cup cherry tomatoes, diced

- Salt and pepper to taste

- 1 tsp olive oil (optional)

Instructions:

1. Toast the slice of whole wheat bread to your liking.

2. Spread the mashed avocado on the toast and top with diced tomatoes.

3. Season with salt and pepper, and drizzle with olive oil if desired.

4. Serve immediately.

Nutritional Info:

- Calories: 220

- Fat: 14g

- Carbs: 22g

- Protein: 5g

5. Cottage Cheese with Pineapple & Walnuts

Prep time: 5 minutes
Cook time: 0 minutes
Total time: 5 minutes

Ingredients:

- 1/2 cup low-fat cottage cheese

- 1/4 cup pineapple chunks (fresh or canned in juice)

- 1 tbsp walnuts, chopped

Instructions:

1. Scoop cottage cheese into a bowl.

2. Top with pineapple chunks and chopped walnuts.

3. Mix and enjoy as a protein-rich, fat-burning snack.

Nutritional Info:

- Calories: 180

- Fat: 10g

- Carbs: 16g

- Protein: 10g

6. Apple Slices with Almond Butter

Prep time: 5 minutes
Cook time: 0 minutes
Total time: 5 minutes

Ingredients:

- 1 medium apple, sliced

- 1 tbsp almond butter

Instructions:

1. Slice the apple into wedges.

2. Serve with almond butter for dipping.

Nutritional Info:

- Calories: 190

- Fat: 14g

- Carbs: 22g

- Protein: 4g

7. Hard-Boiled Eggs with Sea Salt & Pepper

Prep time: 5 minutes
Cook time: 10 minutes
Total time: 15 minutes

Ingredients:

- 2 large eggs

- Sea salt and pepper to taste

Instructions:

1. Place eggs in a pot and cover with water.

2. Bring to a boil, then reduce heat and simmer for 10 minutes.

3. Peel the eggs and sprinkle with sea salt and pepper before serving.

Nutritional Info:

- Calories: 140

- Fat: 10g

- Carbs: 1g

- Protein: 12g

These snacks are designed to keep you energized and satisfied while helping you burn fat throughout the day. They are packed with protein, healthy fats, and fiber—key ingredients to support fat loss and prevent unnecessary snacking on unhealthy options. Keep these simple snacks in your rotation for quick and effective fat-burning results!

Chapter 5: Drinks That Burn Fat

Staying hydrated is essential for fat loss, but certain drinks can do even more to help boost your metabolism and accelerate fat burning. In this chapter, we'll explore seven fat-burning beverages that not only help you stay hydrated but also provide a metabolic boost to help you burn fat faster. These drinks are packed with ingredients known to promote fat loss, such as green tea, apple cider vinegar, and metabolism-boosting herbs. All of them are quick to make and can be incorporated into your daily routine to keep your fat-burning efforts on track.

1. Green Tea Lemonade with Mint

Prep time: 5 minutes
Cook time: 0 minutes
Total time: 5 minutes

Ingredients:

- 1 cup green tea, chilled

- 1 tbsp lemon juice

- 1-2 tsp honey or stevia (optional)

- 1-2 sprigs fresh mint

Instructions:

1. Brew the green tea and let it cool to room temperature or chill in the fridge.

2. In a glass, combine the green tea with lemon juice and sweeten with honey or stevia, if desired.

3. Garnish with fresh mint leaves and stir.

4. Enjoy this refreshing, metabolism-boosting drink!

Nutritional Info:

- Calories: 20

- Fat: 0g

- Carbs: 5g

- Protein: 0g

2. Detoxing Cucumber Water

Prep time: 5 minutes
Cook time: 0 minutes
Total time: 5 minutes

Ingredients:

- 1/2 cucumber, sliced

- 2 cups water

- 1-2 slices lemon (optional)

- 1-2 sprigs fresh mint (optional)

Instructions:

1. Add cucumber slices, lemon slices, and mint sprigs to a large pitcher or glass.

2. Fill with water and stir.

3. Let it infuse for a few minutes, and enjoy this refreshing drink that promotes hydration and digestion.

Nutritional Info:

- Calories: 10

- Fat: 0g

- Carbs: 2g

- Protein: 0g

3. Apple Cider Vinegar Drink with Cinnamon

Prep time: 5 minutes
Cook time: 0 minutes
Total time: 5 minutes

Ingredients:

- 1 tbsp apple cider vinegar

- 1 cup water

- 1/4 tsp cinnamon

- 1 tsp honey or stevia (optional)

Instructions:

1. Combine the apple cider vinegar, water, and cinnamon in a glass.

2. Stir well to dissolve the cinnamon.

3. Sweeten with honey or stevia if desired and enjoy this fat-burning drink!

Nutritional Info:

- Calories: 20

- Fat: 0g

- Carbs: 5g

- Protein: 0g

4. Iced Matcha Latte with Unsweetened Almond Milk

Prep time: 5 minutes
Cook time: 0 minutes
Total time: 5 minutes

Ingredients:

- 1 tsp matcha powder

- 1 cup unsweetened almond milk

- 1/2 tsp vanilla extract

- Ice cubes

- Sweetener of choice (optional)

Instructions:

1. Whisk the matcha powder with a small amount of water to create a smooth paste.

2. Heat almond milk and vanilla extract together, then pour it over ice.

3. Add the matcha paste and stir well.

4. Sweeten with your preferred sweetener, if desired, and enjoy a creamy, fat-burning iced latte!

Nutritional Info:

- Calories: 40

- Fat: 3g

- Carbs: 2g

- Protein: 1g

5. Citrus Fat-Burning Smoothie

Prep time: 5 minutes
Cook time: 0 minutes
Total time: 5 minutes

Ingredients:

- 1/2 orange, peeled

- 1/2 grapefruit, peeled

- 1/4 cup unsweetened almond milk

- 1 tbsp chia seeds

- 1/2 cup ice

Instructions:

1. Blend the orange, grapefruit, almond milk, chia seeds, and ice in a blender until smooth.

2. Pour into a glass and enjoy this refreshing smoothie that helps to boost your metabolism with citrus fruits.

Nutritional Info:

- Calories: 120

- Fat: 5g

- Carbs: 18g

- Protein: 3g

6. Protein-Boosted Coffee Smoothie

Prep time: 5 minutes
Cook time: 0 minutes
Total time: 5 minutes

Ingredients:

- 1 cup brewed coffee, cooled

- 1/2 cup unsweetened almond milk

- 1 scoop protein powder (vanilla or chocolate)

- 1 tsp cinnamon

- Ice cubes

Instructions:

1. In a blender, combine the coffee, almond milk, protein powder, cinnamon, and ice.

2. Blend until smooth and frothy.

3. Enjoy this energizing, fat-burning coffee smoothie!

Nutritional Info:

- Calories: 180

- Fat: 5g

- Carbs: 6g

- Protein: 20g

7. Lemon Ginger Detox Tea

Prep time: 5 minutes
Cook time: 5 minutes
Total time: 10 minutes

Ingredients:

- 1 cup hot water

- 1 tsp freshly grated ginger

- 1 tbsp lemon juice

- 1/2 tsp honey (optional)

Instructions:

1. Boil water and pour it into a mug.

2. Add freshly grated ginger and lemon juice to the hot water.

3. Sweeten with honey if desired and let steep for 2-3 minutes before drinking.

4. Enjoy this detoxifying tea that aids digestion and supports fat loss.

Nutritional Info:

- Calories: 20

- Fat: 0g

- Carbs: 5g

- Protein: 0g

These drinks are designed to enhance fat-burning, aid in digestion, and keep your metabolism revved up throughout the day. They are perfect for sipping between meals, in the morning to start your day, or as a refreshing way to wind down in the evening. Incorporate these beverages into your routine for an added boost to your fat-burning efforts!

Chapter 6: Meal Prep for Success

Meal prepping is one of the most effective strategies for staying on track with your fat-burning goals. By preparing meals in advance, you can save time, reduce stress during the week, and ensure you're always ready with a healthy, fat-burning meal. In this chapter, we'll explore seven meal prep ideas that focus on simple, delicious, and fat-burning ingredients. These recipes can be made in bulk and stored for the week, helping you stay consistent with your fat loss journey.

1. Overnight Oats with Chia and Blueberries

Prep time: 5 minutes
Cook time: 0 minutes (overnight prep)
Total time: 5 minutes

Ingredients:

- 1/2 cup rolled oats

- 1 tbsp chia seeds

- 1/2 cup unsweetened almond milk

- 1/4 cup blueberries

- 1 tsp honey (optional)

- 1/4 tsp cinnamon (optional)

Instructions:

1. In a jar or container, combine oats, chia seeds, almond milk, and cinnamon.

2. Stir well and cover. Let sit in the fridge overnight.

3. In the morning, top with blueberries and a drizzle of honey, if desired.

4. Grab and go for a quick, nutritious breakfast!

Nutritional Info:

- Calories: 200

- Fat: 8g

- Carbs: 30g

- Protein: 6g

2. Chicken & Veggie Stir-Fry (Batch Cooked)

Prep time: 10 minutes
Cook time: 20 minutes
Total time: 30 minutes

Ingredients:

- 2 chicken breasts, cut into strips

- 1 cup broccoli florets

- 1 red bell pepper, sliced

- 1 yellow bell pepper, sliced

- 2 tbsp soy sauce (low-sodium)

- 1 tbsp olive oil

- 1 tsp garlic powder

- 1 tsp ginger, minced

- Salt and pepper to taste

Instructions:

1. Heat olive oil in a large skillet or wok over medium heat.

2. Add chicken strips and cook for 5-7 minutes, until browned and cooked through.

3. Add bell peppers, broccoli, garlic powder, ginger, soy sauce, and salt/pepper.

4. Stir-fry for another 5-7 minutes, until vegetables are tender.

5. Divide into meal prep containers for the week. Reheat when ready to eat.

Nutritional Info:

- Calories: 300

- Fat: 14g

- Carbs: 20g

- Protein: 30g

3. Egg Muffins with Spinach & Feta

Prep time: 5 minutes
Cook time: 15 minutes
Total time: 20 minutes

Ingredients:

- 6 large eggs

- 1/2 cup spinach, chopped

- 1/4 cup feta cheese, crumbled

- Salt and pepper to taste

- Olive oil spray

Instructions:

1. Preheat oven to 350°F (175°C). Spray a muffin tin with olive oil.

2. In a bowl, whisk the eggs and add spinach, feta, salt, and pepper.

3. Pour the egg mixture into muffin cups, filling each about 3/4 full.

4. Bake for 12-15 minutes, until eggs are set.

5. Let cool and store in the fridge for up to 4 days.

Nutritional Info:

- Calories: 120

- Fat: 9g

- Carbs: 3g

- Protein: 9g

4. Sweet Potato & Turkey Chili

Prep time: 10 minutes
Cook time: 30 minutes
Total time: 40 minutes

Ingredients:

- 1 lb ground turkey

- 2 medium sweet potatoes, peeled and diced

- 1 can kidney beans, drained

- 1 can diced tomatoes

- 1 onion, chopped

- 1 tsp chili powder

- 1 tsp cumin

- 1 tsp paprika

- Salt and pepper to taste

Instructions:

1. In a large pot, brown the ground turkey over medium heat.

2. Add onions and cook until softened, about 5 minutes.

3. Stir in sweet potatoes, beans, tomatoes, and spices. Add a pinch of salt and pepper.

4. Cover and simmer for 25-30 minutes, or until sweet potatoes are tender.

5. Divide into containers and store for the week.

Nutritional Info:

- Calories: 350

- Fat: 12g

- Carbs: 35g

- Protein: 28g

5. Kale & Quinoa Salad with Lemon Dressing

Prep time: 10 minutes
Cook time: 15 minutes
Total time: 25 minutes

Ingredients:

- 1 cup quinoa (uncooked)

- 4 cups kale, chopped

- 1/4 cup red onion, thinly sliced

- 1/4 cup cucumber, diced

- 1 tbsp olive oil

- 2 tbsp lemon juice

- Salt and pepper to taste

Instructions:

1. Cook quinoa according to package instructions. Let it cool.

2. In a large bowl, combine kale, red onion, and cucumber.

3. Add cooked quinoa to the salad.

4. Drizzle with olive oil, lemon juice, and season with salt and pepper.

5. Toss to combine and store in meal prep containers.

Nutritional Info:

- Calories: 230

- Fat: 10g

- Carbs: 28g

- Protein: 7g

6. Zucchini Noodles with Bolognese Sauce

Prep time: 5 minutes
Cook time: 20 minutes
Total time: 25 minutes

Ingredients:

- 2 zucchinis, spiralized into noodles

- 1 lb lean ground beef or turkey

- 1 can tomato sauce (low-sodium)

- 1 onion, chopped

- 1 garlic clove, minced

- 1 tsp Italian seasoning

- Salt and pepper to taste

Instructions:

1. Cook ground meat in a pan over medium heat until browned.

2. Add onion and garlic and cook until softened.

3. Stir in tomato sauce, Italian seasoning, salt, and pepper. Simmer for 10 minutes.

4. While the sauce simmers, cook zucchini noodles in a skillet for 3-4 minutes until softened.

5. Top zucchini noodles with the Bolognese sauce and serve immediately or store for meal prep.

Nutritional Info:

- Calories: 300

- Fat: 15g

- Carbs: 15g

- Protein: 25g

7. Grilled Salmon with Roasted Veggies

Prep time: 10 minutes
Cook time: 20 minutes
Total time: 30 minutes

Ingredients:

- 2 salmon fillets

- 1 cup broccoli florets

- 1 cup carrots, sliced

- 1 tbsp olive oil

- Salt and pepper to taste

- Lemon wedges (optional)

Instructions:

1. Preheat the oven to 400°F (200°C). Toss broccoli and carrots with olive oil, salt, and pepper.

2. Roast vegetables on a baking sheet for 15-20 minutes, until tender.

3. Meanwhile, grill or bake salmon fillets for 6-7 minutes per side, or until fully cooked.

4. Serve the salmon with the roasted vegetables and a squeeze of lemon.

Nutritional Info:

- Calories: 350

- Fat: 20g

- Carbs: 12g

- Protein: 35g

These meal prep ideas are designed to help you stay on track with your fat-burning goals by making it easy to prepare and enjoy healthy, satisfying meals throughout the week. With these meals ready to go, you won't have to worry about what to eat, and you'll have more time to focus on your fat loss journey. Enjoy these recipes that support fat-burning while keeping you full and energized!

Chapter 7: Tips for Staying Consistent

Staying consistent is one of the most important factors in achieving long-term fat loss. While quick fixes may provide short-term results, lasting success comes from building sustainable habits that support your goals day after day. In this chapter, we'll cover seven strategies to help you stay consistent with your fat-burning efforts. These tips are designed to help you stay motivated, organized, and on track—no matter what challenges you may face along the way.

1. How to Keep Track of Your Progress

Tracking your progress is key to understanding your journey and staying motivated. Whether you're tracking calories, workouts, or physical measurements, keeping a record allows you to see how far you've come and make adjustments if needed.

Tips for tracking progress:

- **Use an app**: There are many apps available that can help you track your meals, exercise, and even water intake.

- **Take photos**: Sometimes, physical changes are better seen through photos rather than numbers. Take progress photos every few weeks.

- **Measure**: Take measurements of your waist, hips, thighs, and arms to see how your body composition changes over time.

- **Set mini-goals**: Break your bigger fat loss goals into smaller, more achievable targets to celebrate victories along the way.

2. Creating a Weekly Meal Plan That Works

Planning ahead is one of the most effective ways to ensure that you stay on track with your fat-burning goals. A **weekly meal plan** helps you avoid last-minute unhealthy food choices and ensures that you always have nutritious meals ready to go.

Steps to create your weekly meal plan:

- **Plan around your schedule**: If you know you have a busy day, choose simple recipes that require minimal prep time.

For your days off, try new and more complex recipes.

- **Batch cook**: Prepare larger portions of meals like soups, casseroles, or stir-fries to enjoy throughout the week.

- **Snack prep**: Set aside time to prepare snacks in advance so you always have something healthy to grab when hunger strikes.

- **Use leftovers**: Repurpose leftovers for lunches the next day or turn them into something new for dinner.

3. Healthy Eating Habits for Life

Adopting **healthy eating habits** doesn't mean following a restrictive diet for a short period. Instead, focus on creating **sustainable habits** that you can maintain long-term. These habits will help you lose fat and keep it off.

Healthy eating habits to develop:

- **Eat mindfully**: Take time to enjoy your food, chew slowly, and pay attention to your hunger cues.

- **Practice portion control**: Serve your meals on smaller plates to help control portions and prevent overeating.

- **Drink enough water**: Staying hydrated is crucial for fat loss. Aim for at least 8 cups of water per day.

- **Avoid distractions**: Avoid eating in front of the TV or computer, as this can lead to overeating without realizing it.

- **Include protein in every meal**: Protein helps keep you fuller for longer and boosts metabolism.

4. Mindful Eating to Avoid Overeating

Mindful eating is about being present and aware of your body's signals, rather than eating out of habit, stress, or boredom. **Mindful eating** can help you avoid overeating and promote fat loss.

Mindful eating techniques:

- **Eat slowly**: It takes time for your brain to register fullness, so slowing down your eating pace helps prevent overeating.

- **Pay attention to hunger cues**: Eat when you're truly hungry and stop when you feel satisfied—not stuffed.

- **Focus on your food**: Avoid distractions like TV or smartphones while eating. Instead, pay attention to the texture, flavor, and aroma of your food.

- **Use smaller plates**: Eating from smaller plates can help you control portion sizes and prevent overeating.

5. How to Stay Motivated When You're Busy

Life gets hectic, and it can be easy to let healthy habits slip when you're overwhelmed. However, staying consistent with your fat loss goals is possible even when life is busy.

Tips for staying motivated during busy times:

- **Prep meals ahead of time**: Set aside time to meal prep once or twice a week, so you always have healthy meals ready.

- **Keep snacks handy**: Have fat-burning snacks like protein bars, nuts, or fruits on hand for busy days.

- **Set reminders**: Use your phone or a planner to schedule time for meals and workouts.

- **Keep things simple**: On particularly busy days, opt for simple meals like salads, smoothies, or one-pan dinners.

- **Find support**: Share your goals with a friend or family member who can help keep you accountable.

6. Incorporating Exercise with Fat-Burning Meals

Exercise and proper nutrition go hand in hand when it comes to fat loss. **Regular physical activity** not only helps burn calories but also improves overall health and fitness. Combining your healthy meals with consistent exercise will accelerate your fat-burning progress.

Exercise tips for maximizing fat loss:

- **Combine cardio and strength training**: A mix of both will help you burn fat and build lean muscle, which boosts your metabolism.

- **Stay active throughout the day**: Incorporate more movement into your daily routine, like taking the stairs instead of the elevator or going for a brisk walk during lunch.

- **Consistency is key**: Aim for at least 3-4 days of exercise per week. Make it part of your lifestyle, not just a temporary fix.

- **Rest and recover**: Make sure to take rest days to allow your body to recover and repair muscle tissue.

7. Simple Meal Swaps for Fast Results

Making small **meal swaps** can add up to big results over time. Instead of completely overhauling your diet, start with simple, sustainable changes that will support fat loss.

Easy meal swaps to try:

- **Swap white bread for whole wheat or low-carb bread**: Whole grains are higher in fiber and will keep you fuller for longer.

- **Replace sugary snacks with fruits or nuts**: Satisfy your sweet tooth with healthier options like fruit or a handful of almonds.

- **Choose lean protein over fatty cuts of meat**: Opt for chicken, turkey, fish, or plant-based proteins like tofu.

- **Replace creamy dressings with olive oil and vinegar**: A healthier alternative to high-calorie, creamy dressings.

- **Go for roasted or grilled over fried**: Roasting or grilling your food retains more nutrients and cuts down on unnecessary fat.

Staying consistent with your fat loss journey doesn't have to be difficult. By incorporating these strategies into your daily routine, you'll find it easier to stick to your goals and make lasting changes. Remember, consistency is what leads to long-term success, so start small, stay committed, and keep moving forward. Every step you take brings you closer to your fat-burning goals!

Super Fast Fat Burning Cookbook

Chapter 8: Staying Motivated for Long-Term Fat Loss (7 Strategies to Maintain Your Progress)

Motivation is the driving force behind any successful fat loss journey. However, it's natural for motivation to ebb and flow, especially when results aren't immediate or when life gets in the way. This chapter will provide you with seven powerful strategies to keep your motivation high and stay on track for long-term fat loss. By staying motivated, you'll ensure that the healthy habits you've developed become permanent fixtures in your life.

1. Celebrate Small Wins

Staying motivated is easier when you recognize and celebrate the small victories along the way. Achieving fat loss goals doesn't happen overnight, but each step forward is worth celebrating. Whether it's losing a few pounds, fitting into your old jeans, or cooking healthy meals consistently, these small wins help build momentum.

Ways to celebrate small wins:

- **Track your progress**: Keep a journal or use an app to record your achievements and see how far you've come.

- **Treat yourself**: Instead of rewarding yourself with food, treat yourself to something non-food-related like a spa day, new workout gear, or a movie night.

- **Share your success**: Let friends or family know about your achievements. Their encouragement can keep you motivated.

2. Visualize Your Success

Visualization is a powerful tool used by athletes and successful people worldwide. **Visualizing your success** can strengthen your resolve and provide the motivation needed to push through tough moments.

How to use visualization for fat loss:

- **Imagine your goal**: Picture yourself at your goal weight or fitness level, feeling confident and healthy. Visualize how it would feel to wear your favorite clothes or enjoy an active lifestyle.

- **Create a vision board**: Collect images and quotes that inspire you and place them where you can see them every day.

- **Use positive affirmations**: Repeat motivational phrases like "I am strong" or "Every day, I'm getting closer to my goals" to help reinforce your commitment.

3. Stay Accountable to Yourself and Others

Accountability is one of the most effective ways to stay motivated. Whether you're tracking your progress alone or sharing your journey with others, being accountable can help you stay focused on your fat loss goals.

How to stay accountable:

- **Track your food and workouts**: Use apps or a journal to log your meals, workouts, and daily habits. Seeing your progress on paper can be motivating.

- **Join a community**: Whether it's a group on social media, a workout buddy, or an online fat loss group, having others who share similar goals can provide support and encouragement.

- **Tell someone about your goals**: When you share your goals with others, you increase the likelihood of staying committed. Whether it's a friend, partner, or mentor, regular check-ins help keep you on track.

4. Focus on How You Feel, Not Just the Scale

The number on the scale isn't the only measure of progress. Focusing on how you feel physically and mentally can be more motivating than any number. You may experience increased energy, improved mood, or better sleep—all of which are valuable indicators of your progress.

Shift the focus to other indicators of success:

- **Energy levels**: Are you feeling more energized throughout the day? Fat loss isn't just about looking good—it's also about feeling good.

- **Fitness progress**: Celebrate improvements in strength, endurance, or flexibility.

- **Mental clarity**: Many people notice increased focus and less brain fog when they adopt a healthier lifestyle.

5. Set Realistic and Achievable Goals

Setting **realistic and achievable goals** is key to maintaining motivation. Unrealistic expectations can lead to disappointment, while small, attainable goals build confidence and provide regular wins.

How to set achievable fat loss goals:

- **Start with short-term goals**: Focus on losing 1-2 pounds per week, which is a healthy and sustainable rate.

- **Make goals specific**: Rather than saying, "I want to lose weight," aim for something specific like, "I want to lose 5 pounds in 4 weeks."

- **Track your goals**: Break your larger goals into smaller steps and track them weekly. This makes progress feel more manageable and keeps you motivated.

6. Keep a Positive Mindset

A **positive mindset** is essential for long-term success. There will be challenges, and there will be times when things don't go as planned. What matters is how you handle those moments. Maintaining a positive attitude can make the journey more enjoyable and less stressful.

How to stay positive:

- **Embrace the journey**: Fat loss is a process, not a race. Focus on the progress you're making rather than the setbacks.

- **Practice gratitude**: Take time to appreciate what you've accomplished and the small improvements you're making each day.

- **Learn from setbacks**: Instead of being discouraged by challenges, view them as opportunities to learn and grow.

7. Make It Fun

The more **fun** you have with your fat loss journey, the more likely you are to stay motivated. When exercise and healthy eating feel like a chore, motivation can quickly fade. Find ways to make your routine enjoyable and exciting.

How to make fat loss fun:

- **Try new workouts**: Experiment with different activities like dancing, cycling, or swimming. Find something that excites you!

- **Cook creative recipes**: Get creative in the kitchen by trying new fat-burning recipes. Make cooking a fun, relaxing part of your day.

- **Mix up your routine**: Keep things interesting by changing your workouts or meals. This will prevent boredom and keep you engaged.

Staying motivated for long-term fat loss doesn't have to be complicated. By implementing these strategies, you'll build a strong foundation of healthy habits that will help you achieve your fat loss goals and maintain your progress. Remember, success comes from consistent effort, a positive mindset, and a commitment to your well-being. Keep going—you've got this!

Chapter 9: Maintaining Your Results (7 Strategies to Keep the Weight Off)

Achieving fat loss is a significant milestone, but maintaining your results is where the real challenge lies. Long-term weight management requires sustained effort, consistency, and the right mindset. In this chapter, we'll explore seven strategies to help you keep the weight off and continue living a healthy, balanced life without constantly worrying about regaining the pounds you've lost.

1. Keep a Sustainable Routine

After reaching your fat loss goal, it's essential to maintain a routine that supports your new lifestyle. This doesn't mean you have to follow a strict diet forever, but it's important to stay active and mindful of what you eat.

How to keep a sustainable routine:

- **Exercise regularly**: Continue to incorporate physical activity into your routine. Aim for at least 3-4 days of exercise each week.

- **Make healthy eating a habit**: Focus on eating whole, nutrient-dense foods and avoid processed foods. Keep healthy snacks on hand and be mindful of portion sizes.

- **Stay consistent**: Even if you're not actively working to lose more weight, consistency with healthy habits will help maintain your results.

2. Focus on Maintaining Muscle Mass

Muscle mass plays a crucial role in maintaining a healthy metabolism. **Strength training** and staying active help preserve lean muscle, which in turn helps your body burn more calories at rest.

How to preserve muscle mass:

- **Incorporate strength training**: Include weight lifting or bodyweight exercises 2-3 times per week to maintain muscle tone.

- **Protein intake**: Ensure you're consuming enough protein to support muscle repair and growth. Aim for 1.0-1.2 grams of protein per kilogram of body weight.

- **Avoid crash diets**: Rapid weight loss can lead to muscle loss. Aim for slow, steady changes that allow your body to retain muscle while losing fat.

3. Practice Mindful Eating

Mindful eating helps you maintain a healthy relationship with food. It allows you to tune into your hunger and fullness cues, preventing overeating and emotional eating, which are common pitfalls that can lead to weight gain.

Mindful eating practices:

- **Eat slowly**: Take time to enjoy each bite and stop when you're satisfied, not stuffed.

- **Avoid distractions**: Try to eat without the TV or phone, so you can focus on your meal and listen to your body's signals.

- **Check in with yourself**: Before eating, ask yourself if you're truly hungry or if you're eating out of habit, boredom, or stress.

4. Plan for Setbacks

Life is unpredictable, and there will be times when you fall off track. Whether it's due to stress, travel, or a special event, setbacks are a normal part of life. The key is not to let them derail your progress.

How to handle setbacks:

- **Don't be too hard on yourself**: Acknowledge the setback, learn from it, and move on. One mistake doesn't undo all your hard work.

- **Get back to basics**: When you experience a setback, return to your healthy habits—meal prepping, exercising, and staying hydrated.

- **Stay positive**: Focus on the progress you've made, not on any temporary bumps in the road.

5. Keep Track of Your Progress

Regularly tracking your progress helps you stay on track and adjust your habits when needed. Even after reaching your goal, measuring your progress can keep you motivated and ensure that you maintain your results.

Ways to track progress:

- **Weigh yourself regularly**: Weighing yourself once a week (at the same time each day) helps you stay aware of any weight fluctuations.

- **Take measurements**: Measure your waist, hips, and other key areas of your body every month to track changes in body composition.

- **Record your food and activity**: Keep a food diary or use an app to log your meals and workouts, so you can identify patterns and stay accountable.

6. Stay Connected to Your "Why"

Your "why" is the deeper reason behind your fat loss goals. Whether it's to improve your health, feel more confident, or be more active, staying connected to your motivations will help you maintain your results and keep you focused on your long-term success.

How to stay connected to your "why":

- **Revisit your goals**: Regularly remind yourself of why you started your fat loss journey in the first place. Write it down and keep it visible to stay motivated.

- **Visualize your future**: Picture how you'll feel in the long run by maintaining your results. Imagine the benefits—more energy, better health, and increased confidence.

- **Find your support system**: Surround yourself with people who support your goals and remind you of your "why" when things get tough.

7. Maintain a Healthy Relationship with Food

One of the most important aspects of maintaining your weight loss is having a **healthy relationship with food**. This means viewing food as fuel for your body rather than a source of stress or indulgence.

Tips for a healthy relationship with food:

- **Avoid labeling foods as "good" or "bad"**: Instead of categorizing foods, focus on balance and moderation. Treat yourself occasionally, but don't let indulgences derail your progress.

- **Embrace flexible dieting**: It's okay to enjoy your favorite foods in moderation. The key is to incorporate them into an overall healthy eating plan.

- **Focus on balance**: Aim to have a variety of food groups in each meal—protein, carbs, fats, and plenty of fruits and vegetables.

Maintaining your fat loss results isn't about perfection—it's about consistency and finding a balance that works for you. By sticking to these strategies and focusing on long-term sustainable habits, you can keep the weight off for good and continue living a healthy, fulfilling life. Remember, it's not about perfection, it's about progress!

Chapter 11: Final Thoughts and Next Steps

Congratulations on making it this far! By now, you've learned how to eat better, exercise more effectively, and stay consistent with your fat loss journey. But the key to lifelong fat loss isn't just about reaching a goal and stopping—it's about making sustainable changes that support a healthy lifestyle for the long haul. In this final chapter, we'll recap the key takeaways from this book and offer actionable next steps to help you maintain your results, stay motivated, and live your healthiest life.

1. Consistency is Key

One of the most important lessons in fat loss is that **consistency** trumps intensity. While drastic changes can lead to rapid weight loss, those results often don't last without consistency. Small, sustainable habits—like eating balanced meals, exercising regularly, and staying hydrated—build up over time to create lasting change.

Action Step:
Focus on creating a routine that you can maintain long-term. Aim for

consistency with your eating habits, workouts, and overall lifestyle. Start small and gradually build up to bigger challenges.

2. Focus on Health, Not Just Weight Loss

Fat loss is often about more than just looking good—it's about feeling good too. When you shift your focus from **just losing weight** to improving your overall **health and well-being**, it becomes easier to stay motivated and committed. Fat loss is a natural byproduct of taking care of your body, but it's important to remember that your health is the real prize.

Action Step:
 Set health-based goals, such as improving your energy levels, increasing your strength, or achieving better sleep quality. Remember, your body is about more than just the scale—focus on feeling strong, fit, and healthy.

3. Build Healthy Habits for the Long-Term

Sustainable fat loss comes from **building habits** that work with your lifestyle. Instead of focusing on temporary, restrictive diets or workouts, aim to make small, positive changes that fit seamlessly into your daily routine. Healthy habits, such as meal prepping, drinking water, and exercising, will support your long-term fat loss success.

Action Step:
Start by incorporating one or two healthy habits from this book into your routine. For example, try meal prepping for the week or incorporating strength training into your workouts. Build on those habits until they become second nature.

4. Mindset is Everything

The way you think about your fat loss journey has a massive impact on your success. A positive mindset, combined with a **growth-oriented attitude**, will help you overcome obstacles and stay focused on your goals. Remember, setbacks are part of the journey—they don't define your progress. Stay patient, stay focused, and keep going.

Action Step:
Revisit your "why" for fat loss regularly. Write down your motivations, remind yourself of your progress, and use positive

affirmations to stay inspired. Develop a mindset that embraces challenges as opportunities to grow.

5. Embrace Flexibility

While consistency is key, it's equally important to **embrace flexibility** in your fat loss journey. Life happens, and there will be times when you deviate from your plan. Instead of stressing out or feeling guilty, accept that flexibility is part of a balanced, healthy lifestyle. You can always get back on track without perfectionism holding you back.

Action Step:
 Allow yourself to enjoy special occasions or treats in moderation. Practice intuitive eating and focus on your long-term goals rather than short-term slip-ups. Flexibility makes the journey sustainable in the long run.

6. Celebrate Your Progress

Fat loss is a journey, and it's important to acknowledge and celebrate your progress, no matter how small. Every workout completed, every healthy meal prepared, and every pound lost is a step toward your goal. Celebrating your successes keeps you motivated and reinforces the positive behaviors that led to your achievements.

Action Step:
Celebrate each milestone, whether it's losing your first 5 pounds or simply completing a challenging workout. Reward yourself with non-food-related treats, like a relaxing bath, a new workout outfit, or a fun activity that makes you feel proud.

7. Keep Learning and Evolving

Fat loss is not a one-time event; it's an ongoing journey of learning and evolving. As you continue on your path to better health, you'll gain new insights about your body, your habits, and your preferences. Stay open to experimenting with new workouts, healthy recipes, and personal growth strategies. The more you learn, the more equipped you'll be to maintain your results.

Action Step:
Keep reading, exploring, and educating yourself on topics related to nutrition, fitness, and wellness. Stay open to trying new strategies, and be willing to adjust your approach as you grow. Lifelong fat loss is about continuous improvement, not perfection.

Next Steps: Take Action Now

Now that you've completed the *Super Fast Fat Burning Cookbook*, it's time to take action! Here are a few next steps to help you put everything you've learned into practice:

1. **Create a Meal Plan**: Choose a few recipes from the book and create your meal plan for the week. Prepare your meals ahead of time to make healthy eating easy and convenient.

2. **Start Small**: Focus on one or two habits at a time—whether it's exercising regularly, drinking more water, or meal prepping. Gradually build upon these habits for sustainable progress.

3. **Track Your Progress**: Start tracking your meals, workouts, and any other goals you have set for yourself. Use an app or journal to stay accountable and see how far you've come.

4. **Join a Community**: Surround yourself with like-minded individuals who share your goals. Whether online or in person, find a group or partner to keep you motivated and accountable.

5. **Be Consistent**: The most important step is to take consistent action. Whether it's cooking healthy meals, exercising, or practicing mindful eating, stick with it and

trust the process.

Conclusion: Your Journey Begins Now

Congratulations again on completing the *Super Fast Fat Burning Cookbook!* By now, you have the tools and knowledge to take control of your fat loss journey. Remember, fat loss is not a sprint—it's a marathon. Stay patient, stay consistent, and keep moving forward. With the right mindset and habits, you can achieve lasting success and maintain your results for life.

Now, it's time to take the first step. Your transformation begins today. Go ahead, make it happen!

Printed in Great Britain
by Amazon

62828083R00067